Everything You Need to Know About

Credit Cards and Fiscal Responsibility

Get Cash

Learn about handling your money
early so you won't end up in debt!

Everything You Need to Know About

Credit Cards and Fiscal Responsibility

Meg Green

The Rosen Publishing Group, Inc.
New York

To my husband, Todd Dawson. Without his support,
this book would not have been possible.

Published in 2001 by The Rosen Publishing Group, Inc.
29 East 21st Street, New York, NY 10010

Library of Congress Cataloging-in-Publication Data

Green, Meg.
    Everything you need to know about credit cards and fiscal responsibility / Meg Green. — 1st ed.
    p. cm. — (Need to know library)
ISBN: 978-1-4358-8686-5
1. Credit cards—United States—Juvenile literature. 2. Bank credit cards—United States—Juvenile literature. [1. Credit cards. 2. Finance, personal.] I. Title. II. Series.
HG3755.8.U6 G74   2000
332.7'65—dc21

00-010321

Manufactured in the United States of America

Contents

Introduction

Visa. MasterCard. American Express. They are credit cards, and everyone wants one. You see people use them in movies and on television, in magazines and in real life. People see something they want, and with a credit card, they get it. A credit card is like a genie, but there seems to be no limit to the number of wishes it can grant.

Credit cards seem like a one-way ticket to paradise, giving you the power to buy, buy, buy whatever you desire. A flick of the wrist, and you can have a new computer or video game. Just sign on the line and walk out with your brand-new compact disc or gold chain. Put the card in a machine, and out pour crisp new twenty-dollar bills.

The Lure of Easy Money

The message from the credit card companies seems to be: Don't worry about paying for it today. You'll pay for it tomorrow. And the day after tomorrow. And the day after that. That's the problem. Put it on plastic, and you may end up paying four or five times more tomorrow than you would if you had just paid cash today. The reality is that credit cards are not magic, and they are not free. They are loans, and loans must be paid back. If you do not pay them back, there are serious consequences that can hurt you in the future.

Credit cards, also called charge cards, were started by a hapless businessman who forgot his wallet one night when he went out to dinner. His wife paid for the meal, but the businessman thought it would be convenient if he could just show the restaurant a card that could prove he would pay his bill even if he didn't have cash on hand. And so the Diners Club card, the first credit card, was born.

To get a credit card, you must sign a contract with a bank or another lender, sometimes a store. The credit card company promises to loan you a limited amount of money when you use the card. In return, you promise to pay back the amount you borrowed, plus interest. Interest is what the credit card company charges you to borrow the money, and it can add up fast.

While credit cards can be a one-way ticket to debt, if used carefully, they can be a helpful tool. They can get your car fixed in an emergency when you are away from home, or they can help you buy something that you need today but can't afford to pay cash for all at once. They can also help you fight when you are not happy with the product or service you purchased from a merchant.

Also, if you use a credit card wisely, you will build a strong credit history. Credit history is a record of your financial responsibility, and banks and other lenders will consider that history when you apply for a loan to buy a house or a car.

If you are going to be smart about credit cards, you must first know the rules. This book will show you what you need to know so you will be the master of your cards, not the other way around. Let's go over the basics.

Chapter One

The Basics: How Credit Cards Work

When you use your credit card to buy something in a store, the clerk swipes your card through a machine and asks you to sign for the purchase. This is your promise to pay the bill later, when it is mailed to your home. You walk away with what you bought, while your credit card company pays the store within a few days of the transaction. The credit card company has loaned you the money for the purchase you just made. You can also give out your card number over the phone to buy something from a catalog, or you can punch it into your computer to buy something via the Internet. These purchases don't require a signature.

At the end of the next billing period, usually about a month, the credit card company sends you a bill that

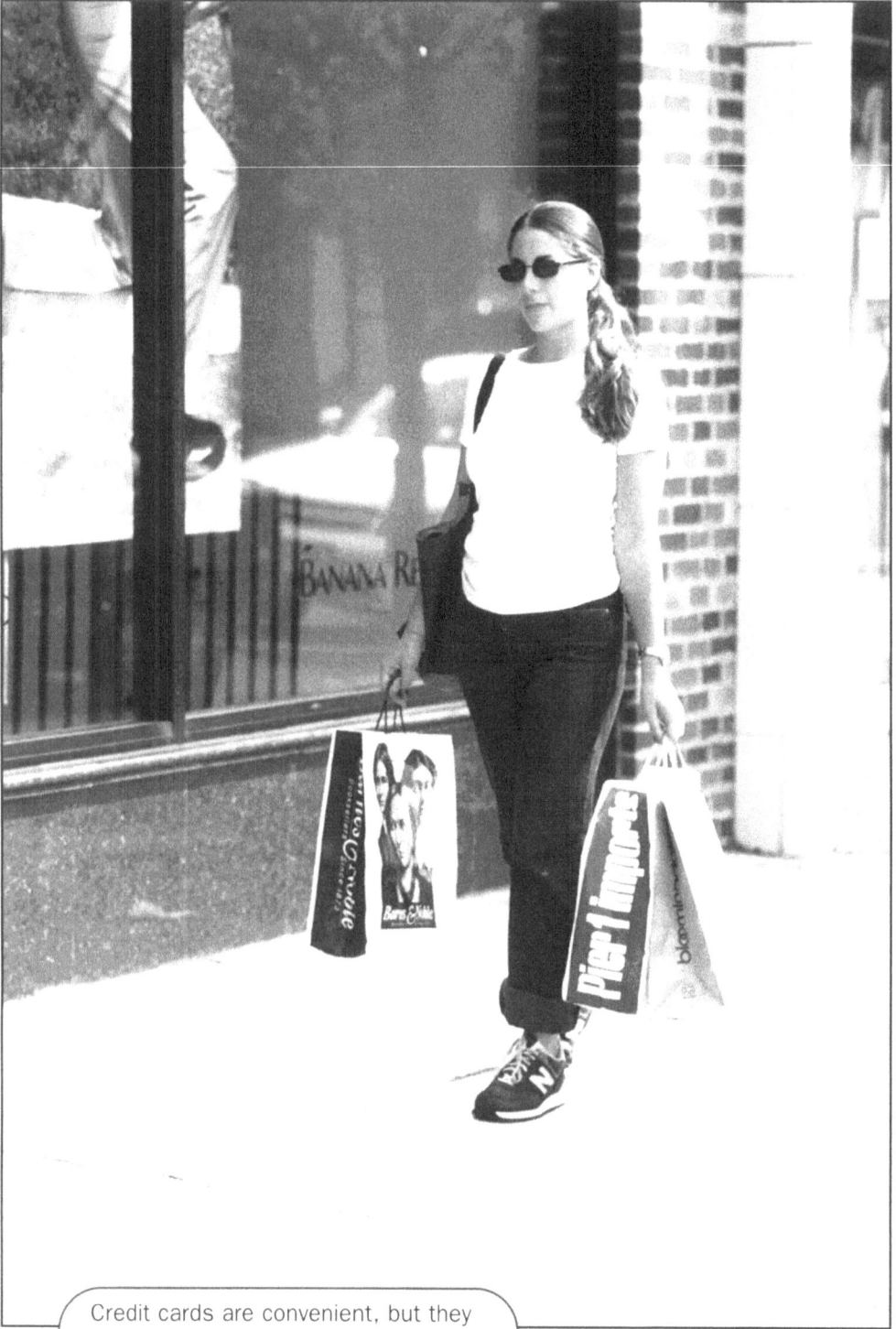

Credit cards are convenient, but they also make it very easy to overspend.

shows what you have purchased, plus a lot of other important information you need to know, such as any unpaid balance, the total amount that you owe, any interest charged, what your minimum payment is, and when it is due.

Falling into Debt

Using credit cards can be very tempting because they allow us to think in terms of monthly payments, instead of how much something really costs at the moment of purchase. Maybe you can't afford to buy a $3,000 item up-front, but you think you can afford to pay $30 a month. Let's say you see an incredible, top-of-the-line computer system that you absolutely "must" have. It's $3,000. You don't have that kind of cash but decide to buy it with a credit card and pay it off a little every month.

If you carry a $3,000 balance on a credit card with a 19 percent interest rate and pay the required minimum balance of 2 percent each month, or $15 (whichever is less), it would take you thirty-six years to pay off the loan. That's because the minimum payment barely covers the cost of interest. And, what is worse, when you finally pay off that computer after thirty-six years, you will have paid about $9,300 in interest charges alone. Yikes! That means you will have paid a total of $12,300, which is more than four

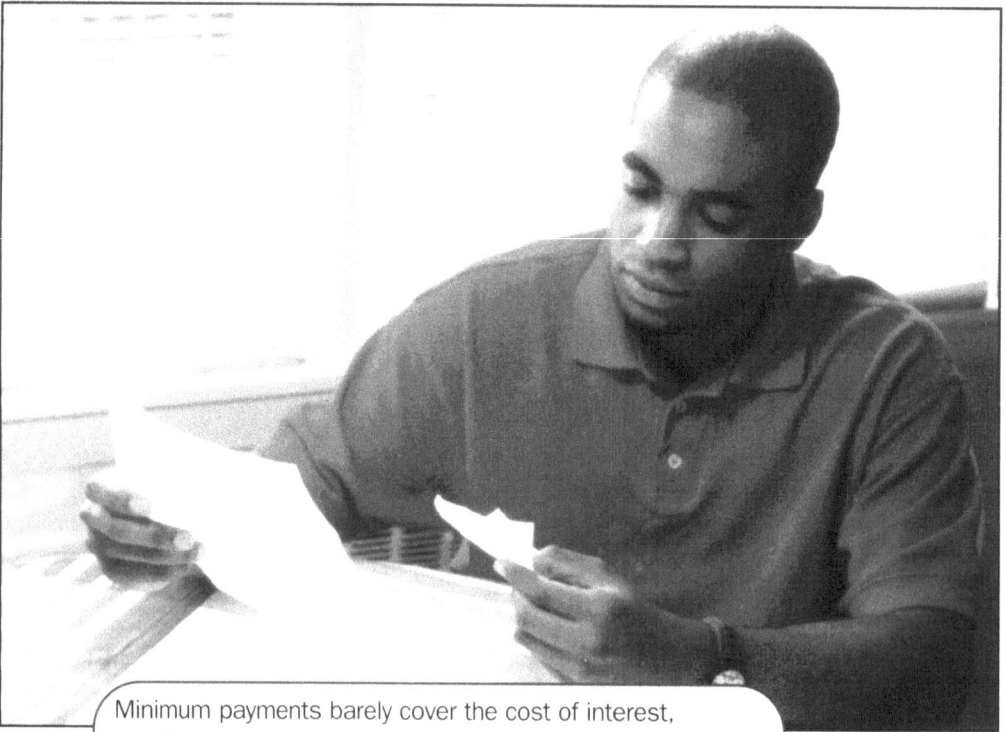

Minimum payments barely cover the cost of interest, causing the purchase price of an item to multiply over time.

times the cost of the $3,000 computer. Okay, so maybe you have no plans to spend $3,000 all at once. But people can also run up credit card bills quickly just by making smaller purchases, which with interest can add up quickly.

About twenty-six cents of every dollar spent in America on discretionary spending (that's not related to necessities like groceries or housing) is put on plastic, according to CardWeb.com. That means more than a quarter of all money spent on fun things—like movies, fast food, and compact discs—is being paid for with a loan.

Credit card spending in the United States has more than doubled in eight years, growing from $172.6 billion in 1990 to $454.3 billion in 1998. The average American household with at least one credit card carried a credit card debt of $7,564 in 1999, up from an average of $2,985 in 1990.

Targeting Young Buyers

Credit card companies are targeting young people more today than ever before. You must be eighteen, a legal adult, to be able to sign a legal contract needed to get a credit card. However, some kids get their own cards through their parents' account or through another adult co-signing the contract. Once you are eighteen, you can get your own card without your parents' permission.

About six million undergraduate college students have credit cards, according to one survey. About two out of three students have at least one credit card, while 27 percent have four or more cards. One in four students received his or her first card in high school. The average credit card balance, or debt, per student is $1,879. If a first-year student runs up a $1,000 bill on a credit card with a 14 percent interest rate, and pays only the monthly minimum payment, it will take nine years to pay off that freshman year debt. And that's if the credit card was not used to buy anything else!

By signing the original contract to get the card in the first place, you are also agreeing to pay the bill when it comes. There are lots of credit cards, and cards that only look like credit cards. Here's how they are different.

The Many Breeds of Credit Cards

- Bank credit cards are issued by individual banks under a large corporate name, such as Visa, MasterCard, and Discover. Terms and conditions can change depending on the bank that issued the card. You can carry a balance, or debt, on your card, but you are required to make payments, usually every month. These are the most common types of cards, usually called major credit cards.

- Charge cards, like American Express, expect you to pay off your entire balance every month.

- House cards are good only at the store that issued the card. For instance, Macy's isn't going to accept your Sears card and Texaco won't take your Exxon card. There are some exceptions where stores share the same corporate parent or have made arrangements to share house cards.

Some Cards Need an Anchor

Cards are further divided into what kind of collateral—proof that you will be able to pay your bills—

the bank or issuing store expects from you, the customer. Remember, the credit card companies are not giving away money; they expect you to pay it back!

- Unsecured cards are the most common type of card, usually just known as credit cards. The bank or issuer of the card doesn't expect you to put up any money up front and guarantees to loan you a limited amount of money whenever you need it. In return, you sign a contract promising to pay the bills when they come, even if it means just making a partial payment. Often the cards come with a personal identification number, or PIN, so you can use the cards in an automatic teller machine (ATM) to withdraw a cash advance. Memorize your PIN, and don't write it down and keep it with your card. You don't want thieves to find your card and know how to get instant cash with it!

♦ Debit cards are issued by banks in connection with a checking or savings account you have with that specific bank. Like a regular credit card, debit cards have a Visa or MasterCard symbol on them, and you can use debit cards anywhere that Visa or MasterCard is accepted. Visa calls its debit card a Visa Check Card, and MasterCard calls its card a Mastermoney Card.

Unlike a credit card, when you use your debit card at a store, the bank deducts your purchases from your checking or savings account immediately. Because the money is coming directly from your own account, you won't get a monthly bill. Your debit card purchases will show up on your monthly bank statements, just like any checks or withdrawals you make. You can also use your debit card to access money from your accounts from automatic teller machines using your PIN.

At some stores, you will be asked to sign for your purchase, just as if you had used a credit card. This is called an off-line transaction. Sometimes you will have to punch your PIN into a machine to approve the transaction. This is called an on-line transaction. More stores have machines that read credit cards than have machines that accept PIN numbers.

* ATM cards, or automatic teller machine cards, are issued by banks and allow users to take cash out of their bank accounts using ATMs. This card does not have a Visa or MasterCard symbol on it, and you cannot use it as a charge card. You can use it at some stores that are equipped with special machines that allow you to type in your PIN to deduct money directly from your account.

* Secured cards are issued by banks that require you to make a bank deposit to get the card. A secured card is sort of a combination between an unsecured, or regular, card and a debit card. Like a credit card, you get billed for your purchases. But if you don't pay your bill, the bank can take the money directly from your account.

* Guaranteed cards are similar to secured cards, but you usually have to pay an application fee

or use an expensive 900-number to get them, so they are rarely a good deal.

To make it even more confusing, two different Visa cards can have different contracts, so one could be twice as expensive to use. How can you tell a good card deal from a bad one? Usually it involves reading the small print that comes with the credit card contract. In the next chapter, we'll go over the basic contract terms to see inside credit card plans.

Chapter Two

Fine Print: The Good, the Bad, and the Ugly

Few people enjoy reading the complicated legal stuff in contracts. The print is usually small, there are often a lot of big words, and the writing itself is so dry it might put you to sleep. It's like a textbook for the most boring class in the world. However, as dreadful as it is to read, it is in the boring fine print that you will discover important things about your card, and how much it will cost you to use it.

"Most people don't read the applications before they fill them out," says Steve Rhode, president of Myvesta.org, a nonprofit organization that helps people get out of debt. "They get so excited. They need to understand that just because you got an application in the mail, it doesn't mean you can afford the card." Let's look at some of the common terms you'll find in your credit card contract and also in any monthly credit card bill.

VISA® APPLICATION

VISA

CROSS COUNTRY

□ **YES!** Please p
application for an U S
VISA Credit Card

I understand that my acco
will be a minimum of $
that the VISA Applicatio
Fee along with the Ann
charged to my account
card has been issued

Please make any necessary name or address corrections below:

083   4000398051050 0
Penny Turner
325 Shore Rd. Apt. 1E
Long Beach, NY 115

□ **EXPRESS SERVICE**
bank receives my

Copy of a recent b

rd mailed to me in as little as ten bus
charge $10 to my card.

bill does not need to be in your
bill are required with this ap
cation will not be processed

YOURSELF

IF YOU ARE RELYING ON SO

COMPLETE

TANCE AND SIGN

CAP ENROLLMENT FOR
YES! Please enroll

I will be sent a Credit Card Applicati
Agreement. You have engaged Applica
about us and we my access loan react
rate and exchange cards advances wire
minimum

X_____
Applicant's Signature

X_____
Driver's License Number

PLEASE INCLUDE PROOF OF V

VISA is a registered trademark of VISA

Interest is a percentage of money you must pay to a credit card company for using your credit card. It can vary widely from lender to lender, and can even change once you have established an account with the lender. It's a very basic term, which is further divided into the annual percentage rate and periodic rate.

Annual percentage rate (APR) is how much interest will be charged in a year. It's a percentage that is added to the money you have borrowed. But unless you get only one bill a year, the number is theoretical. You can compare different companies' APRs, but keep your eye on the periodic rate.

Periodic rate is the interest charged in a billing period, and it is a more practical number to keep track of. If the credit card company sends out twelve bills a year, the periodic rate is the APR divided by 12. For instance, a credit card with an APR of 21 percent would have a monthly periodic rate of 1.75 percent.

What does it all mean? Putting a $1,000 charge on a card with a 21 percent APR and a periodic rate of 1.75 percent would mean you'd pay $210 in interest for a year and $17.50 for a month. The interest for a year isn't completely accurate, though, because it doesn't take into account compound interest. We'll explain that in the next chapter.

Be Interested in Interest

Pay attention to interest because the higher the interest rate, the more expensive it can be to use your card. See

The Interest Chart

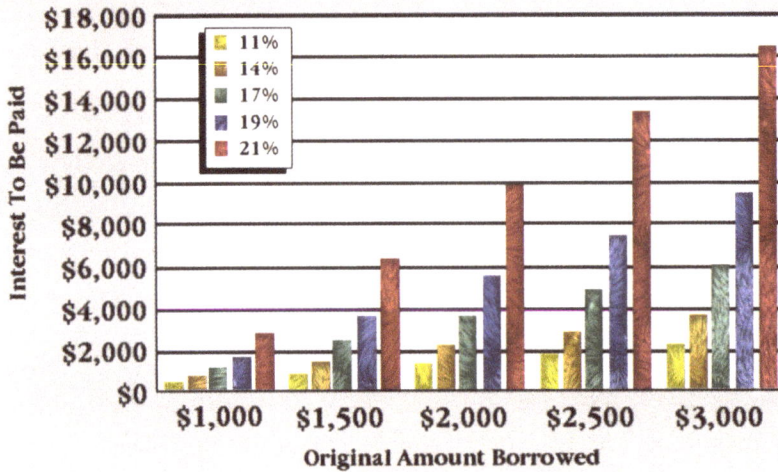

Chart title: **The Interest Chart**

Y-axis: Interest To Be Paid ($0, $2,000, $4,000, $6,000, $8,000, $10,000, $12,000, $14,000, $16,000, $18,000)

Legend:
- 11%
- 14%
- 17%
- 19%
- 21%

X-axis: Original Amount Borrowed ($1,000, $1,500, $2,000, $2,500, $3,000)

As you borrow more money, your interest amounts increase correspondingly.

how the dollars you pay in interest increase as the percentage of interest increases? See how the interest you pay grows as you borrow more, and how it grows as the rates grow? This is if you only pay the minimum payment, or $15 a month, whichever is less.

Saving Grace

Low interest rates are good, high interest rates are bad. But for many cards, there is a way of escaping paying interest at all—by paying off your total bill every month. Remember, however, if you do that, the card company won't make any money off you, so they are not going to spell this option out for you in their contract or mailings. What to look for? The grace period.

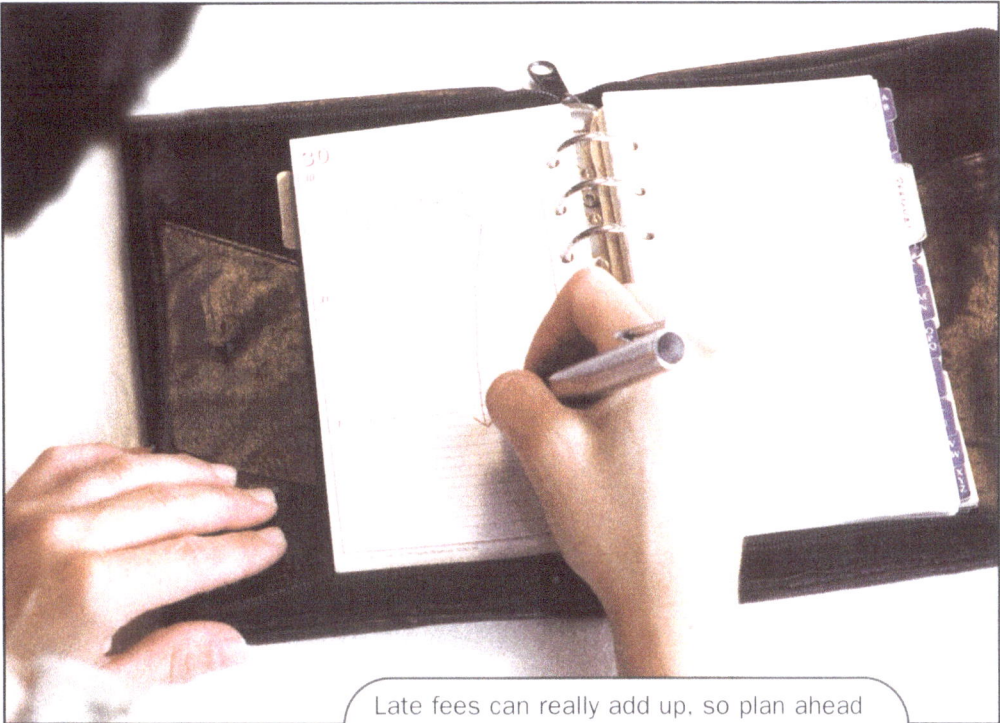

Late fees can really add up, so plan ahead to make sure that you pay your bills on time.

A grace period is how much time a credit card company allows you to carry a debt without charging interest on it. For instance, if you use your card to buy new sneakers, you can carry that charge on your account for about twenty to twenty-five days before the credit card company will charge interest on the purchase. With a grace period, if you pay off your credit card bills every month, you might not have to pay interest at all on your purchases. However, if you don't pay off your bill every month, your grace period disappears. That means if you carry a balance on your bill, any new purchases are charged interest from the moment you make them. Also, be wary of cash advances because they usually don't get grace periods at all.

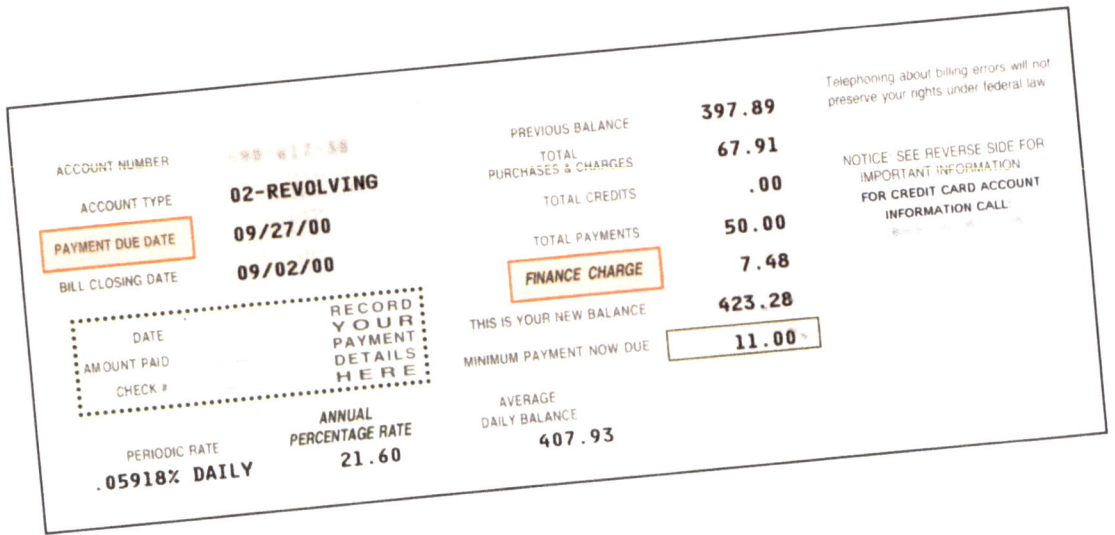

ACCOUNT NUMBER		PREVIOUS BALANCE 397.89	Telephoning about billing errors will not preserve your rights under federal law
ACCOUNT TYPE **02-REVOLVING**	TOTAL PURCHASES & CHARGES 67.91	NOTICE SEE REVERSE SIDE FOR IMPORTANT INFORMATION
PAYMENT DUE DATE **09/27/00**	TOTAL CREDITS .00	FOR CREDIT CARD ACCOUNT INFORMATION CALL
BILL CLOSING DATE **09/02/00**	TOTAL PAYMENTS 50.00	

FINANCE CHARGE 7.48

THIS IS YOUR NEW BALANCE 423.28

MINIMUM PAYMENT NOW DUE 11.00

RECORD YOUR PAYMENT DETAILS HERE

DATE
AMOUNT PAID
CHECK #

ANNUAL PERCENTAGE RATE 21.60

AVERAGE DAILY BALANCE 407.93

PERIODIC RATE .05918% DAILY

> Examine your credit card bills carefully to understand the finance charges, interest rates, and credit limits.

Here are some other terms that credit card companies use:

- Finance charge is what it costs to use the card. It can include other charges, such as cash advance fees, late fees, and so on.

- Limit or credit line is the dollar amount the company is willing to loan you. For a secured card, it is the amount you have in your account. For a regular credit card, it can vary depending on how responsible the company thinks you are.

- Credit available is the amount of credit you haven't used yet. It is the amount of your limit minus your balance.

◆ Payment due date is when the credit card company must receive your payment. If you are late, you could face an additional fee. A word of advice: The date is when the company wants your check in hand, not postmarked and in the mail. Plan ahead and make sure your bills are paid on time.

Fee Circus

Credit card companies have lots of ways to make you pay additional money to them through fees. Here are some to look out for:

◆ Annual fee is the amount per year the lender is charging you for the privilege of carrying its credit card in your wallet, even if you never use it. Annual fees can range from $15 to $55, but some cards don't charge an annual fee at all.

◆ Cash advance fees are the charges a lender levies on you when you use its card in an ATM to get cash, or write a check on your credit card account. These little fees can make borrowing cash from your credit card company a very expensive proposition. Cash advances can also come with a higher interest rate than other purchases on your card.

◆ Late fees are levied on you if you don't get your payment to the credit card company on time.

◆ Over-limit fee is a charge levied on you when you borrow over your limit. You can run over your limit and not even know it. Interest rates, late fees, and other charges can push you over your limit and trigger the over-limit fee. Some cards will stop you from borrowing over your limit and reject any attempted purchases you make over the limit. Others will let you make the purchase but then charge you for being over the limit.

The Ugly

How do credit card companies actually figure out what interest you owe? It's a little like making soup: lots of different things are thrown in the mix, and companies come up with different amounts even when they charge you the same interest rate. The following are some of the methods they use:

◆ Outstanding balance method means if you haven't paid off your full balance before the grace period expires, you will pay interest on the unpaid balance and any new purchases you made after that. Your new purchases will be charged interest from the day you put them on your card—there's no grace period for them.

◆ Average daily balance method involves adding up all of the debt on your card in the billing period, and dividing it by the number of days in the period to get an average amount owed on your card on any day in the period. Then the interest rate is applied to that average number and added to your total bill.

♦ Two-cycle, or multiple cycle, system is the worst billing system for consumers. Under this system, the credit card company divides a month into two cycles, or billing periods. Say the month is split from the 1st to the 15th, and from the 15th to the end of the month. If you make a purchase on the 14th, the credit card company can begin charging you interest on the 15th, the first day of the second cycle. You will end up paying more interest this way.

Whew! Congratulations on making it through the mumbo jumbo of fine print. This is a lot of information to digest, but you are probably still wondering how credit cards can be so expensive. Let's see how credit card companies charge interest.

The final price of an expensive mountain bike can nearly double if you make minimum payments at a high APR.

Chapter Three

Plastic Is Not Cheap

Credit cards are a great convenience because they let you enjoy something today and pay for it tomorrow. But credit cards are a type of loan, and they come with a cost. You must pay back what you borrow, plus interest and any additional fees the lender charges you. Carrying a balance is expensive because credit card companies can charge you interest on what you borrowed, plus if you carry a balance for several months or longer, they charge interest on the interest they have already calculated. That is called compound interest.

Albert Einstein called compound interest the most powerful thing he had ever seen. Let's see why. Say you celebrate your eighteenth birthday by buying a new mountain bike for $2,000. You put the purchase on a credit card with an 18 percent APR and a thirty-day grace period. Your first month's credit card bill will have a balance of $2,000—just your original purchase, with no interest charge, because you are still in the grace period. The minimum payment is 2 percent of your balance, or $40. You decide to pay just the minimum payment of $40.

It sounds like a bargain, right? You're out and about, riding your new bike, having a great time, and you had to pay only $40! But you are not done paying yet. In the second month, you might think your unpaid balance should be $1,960 (that's your $2,000 bike minus the $40 payment you made last month). Not so fast—this time, you must pay an interest charge, too.

To figure out the interest charge, your credit card company takes your 18 percent APR and divides it by twelve to get your monthly periodic rate, or 1.5 percent. Then your outstanding balance, or unpaid bill, is multiplied by the monthly interest rate: $1,960 x 1.5 percent = $30. That $30 of interest is added to your balance of $1,960 to get a total bill of $1,990. So you still owe $1,990. That means $30 of your $40 first payment went toward interest, and only $10 went to pay down your principal, or original purchase. You decide to pay only the minimum payment again, which is $39.80 (It's a little less this time, but not much).

To calculate your third monthly bill, the credit card company takes the balance for the second month, $1,990, and subtracts your payment of $39.80. That gives you a new balance of $1,950.20, which is multiplied by 1.5 percent to get an interest charge of $29.25, which is added

Cost of Bike $2,000.00
My first payment – $40.00
$1,960.00
+ $30.00
Interest
New balance $1,990.00
My second payment – $39.80
$1,950.20
+ $29.25
Interest
New balance $1,979.45

Total that I put in:
$79.80
Total off the bill:
$20.55

to your balance. That gives you a new total of $1,979.45. So although you have already paid $79.80 in cash for your new bike, your credit card debt has decreased only by $20.55. You are barely making headway in paying down the debt.

Why is that? Because most credit cards' minimum payments barely cover the interest charged. With compound interest you take a step back for every two steps forward.

But who cares? You still have your bike, right? Well, if you continue to make just the minimum payment required every month, you would be forty-two by the time you paid off your bike. That's not a typo. It will take you more than twenty-four years to pay off that debt. When you do finally pay it off, you will have paid $4,396.66 in interest alone. Remember, this is if all you do is make a one-time purchase of $2,000 and make the minimum payment each month. And this is also if you make every payment on time and are not charged additional late fees or use the card to buy anything else in that twenty-four-year period.

The Interest and Time Chart

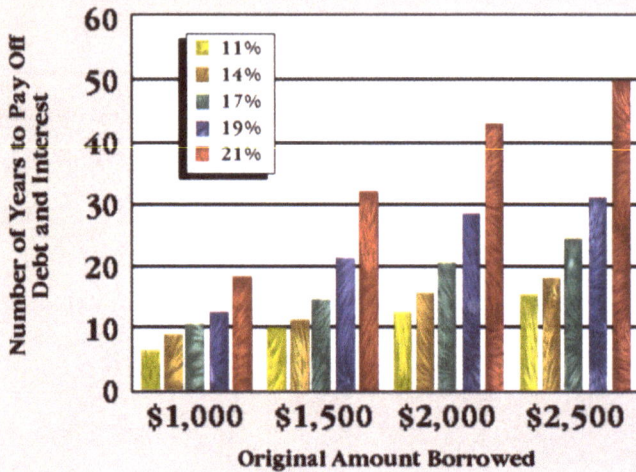

Number of Years to Pay Off Debt and Interest (y-axis)

Legend:
- 11%
- 14%
- 17%
- 19%
- 21%

Original Amount Borrowed (x-axis): $1,000 $1,500 $2,000 $2,500

It can take years to pay off credit card debt through minimum monthly payments, depending on the interest rate.

Time Is Money

Michael T. Killian, a financial advisor who hosts a Web site at About.com, warns teens—and adults—about the dangers of credit cards. "It is so easy to think, 'I'm not spending anything, this is plastic,'" Killian says. "Remember, this is real money. Pay it off as rapidly as possible. You are selling your future away if you make only the minimum payment."

Compound interest is an enemy when you are paying it to a credit card company. However, you can harness the power of compound interest yourself by saving and investing money. If you had taken that $4,396.66 in interest and invested it in a mutual fund with a 10 percent return, you would have $47,985.57 in twenty-four years.

Use your credit wisely—charge moderately priced items and make payments quickly.

Most financial advisors will tell you not to use a credit card to buy something you can't quickly pay off. However, credit cards can be a good deal if you use them wisely. For instance, you can use that same 18 percent APR card to buy a $100 compact disc player. Your first bill comes and you owe $100. There is no interest yet because you are still in the grace period. The minimum payment is $15, but you know it's smart to pay more than the minimum, so you pay $50. Next month, your unpaid balance is $50, plus an interest charge of $0.75. If you pay the $50.75 now, you will have paid a total of only $100.75 for the compact disc player. Using your credit card gave you more time to pay it off, and it cost you only an extra seventy-five cents. You also made sure you could pay off the entire bill before making any additional purchases.

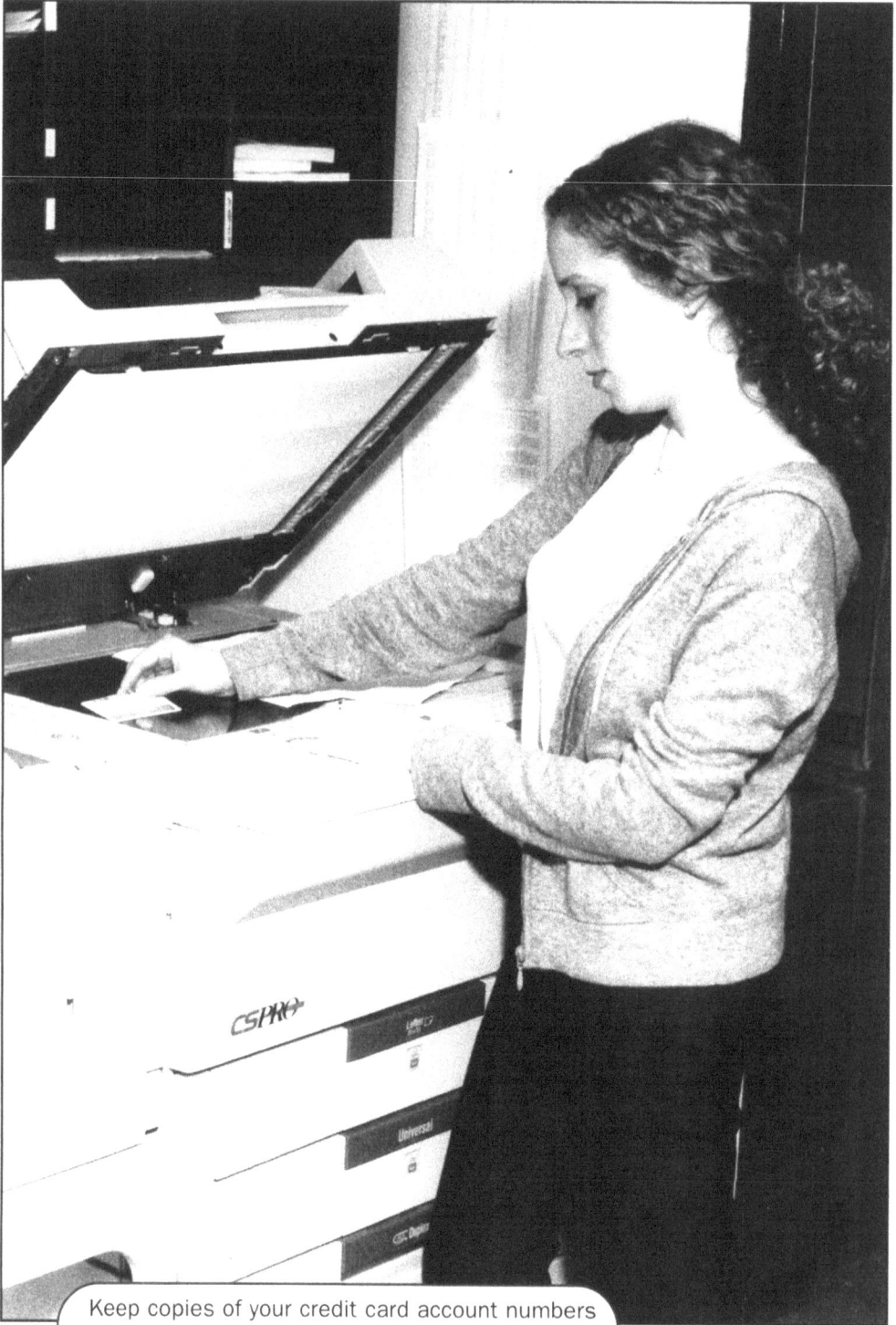

Keep copies of your credit card account numbers in case you have to report a lost or stolen card.

Chapter Four

Your Credit History: How Responsible Are You?

You may think it is no one else's business whether you pay your bills on time, or how much you pay. You may think no one else should know about your private business with credit card companies and other institutions. The truth is that other people do know, and they will know in the future, too.

Your credit history is your financial reputation and a measure of how responsible you are. When you apply for a credit card or other loan, the credit card company or bank investigates you to see how likely it is that you will pay your debt. Just like in school, you will be graded. Do you pay your bills on time? How much money do you owe? Do you have a good job? To check your credit history, companies will check your credit report and see how worthy you are by investigating the three C's of credit.

The Three C's of Credit

- **Capacity**—how much can you borrow? It is your ability to pay based on your income, or how much money you make, and your existing debt, or how much you owe.

- **Character**—how trustworthy are you? It refers to things like how long you have been employed and whether you pay your bills on time.

- **Collateral**—do you have anything of value? It refers to any assets you have that prove you are financially stable, such as a house or a bank account.

It's important to know what is in your credit history because sometimes the credit reporting agencies make mistakes. You don't want your reputation tarnished by someone else's error. Your own errors will stay on your record for some time, up to seven years. Missing payments, late payments, and other problems can tarnish your record long after you've forgotten about them. Believe it or not, bankruptcy stays on your report for ten years.

What Is Your Credit Record?

Financial advisors recommend you check your credit history every one to three years. How do you do that? There are three main credit bureaus, also called consumer reporting agencies, that banks, stores, and credit

A poor credit rating can affect you negatively; your card may be denied for some purchases.

card companies report to. They keep track of consumers and how they use credit. Do they pay their bills on time? How many credit cards do they have? How much debt do they have?

Not all businesses report to all three agencies, so they don't always have the same information on the same people. It is wise to request reports from all three. If you applied for credit and were turned down, you are allowed a free copy of your credit report if you respond within thirty days of the denial. Otherwise, the reporting agencies charge a small fee for copies of credit reports.

Requests for credit reports should include your signature and check or money order to pay for the report. If you ask for the fee to be waived because of a recent credit denial, you must include a copy of the letter that denied you credit. You should also include your full name, current address and addresses for the last five years, daytime phone number, date of birth, social security number, and a photocopy of a credit card statement, utility bill, driver's license, or another document that shows your name and address.

If you see something in your report that doesn't make sense or should not be there, you should contact the credit bureau. If you think someone has wrongfully used your name to apply for credit, you can call the National Fraud Information Center's customer assistance program from 8:30 AM to 5:30 PM EST at (800) 876-7060.

Building Your Credit History

Sometimes it is easy for teens to get a credit card even without a solid credit history because credit card companies figure that teens will eventually pay off the debt, even if their parents have to help. But often, if you have no credit history because you've never taken a loan for a car or another big purchase, you may have to build a credit history before you can get a card. To do that, consider applying for a credit card at a local store, and ask if the store reports to a credit bureau. If it does, and you are responsible and pay your bills on time, you'll be well on your way to establishing a good credit history.

Credit Bureaus

EQUIFAX

(800) 997-2493
Web site: http://www.equifax.com
Cost of report: $8

EXPERIAN

(888) 397-3742
Web site: http://www.experian.com
Cost of report: $8 in most states

TRANSUNION

Consumer Disclosure Center
(800) 888-4213
Web site: http://www.transunion.com
Cost of report: $8

A consolidated report on the information gathered by the major bureaus can be ordered from:

FIRST AMERICAN CREDCO

(800) 443-9342
Web site: http://facredco.com
Cost of report: $29.95

You can also consider applying for a secured card. By putting a deposit down for collateral, you can get a credit card based on the amount you put down, usually 50 to 100 percent of your deposit. You may face more charges and higher interest rates than a regular credit card, but if you responsibly use your secured credit card, you can reapply for a regular credit card in the future. You may also want to consider asking your parents or another adult to co-sign an application for you. Be careful. The cosigner promises to pay your bills if you do not. Still, if you responsibly use the card and pay your bills on time, you will be building your own credit history. If you run up a debt and force your cosigner to pay, you will be hurting your own credit history, while probably upsetting your cosigner.

Steve Rhode from Myvesta.org recommends that teens get a secured card with their parents' cosignature. "We live in a credit society. Credit is a privilege, not a right," Rhode says. "Parents should give their kids cards with training wheels. Let them earn enough money to put up their own money. Now is the time to teach them about personal financial management."

Apply for just one card at a time. Credit bureaus keep track of every company that asks about you, and some companies may turn down your application if they think you are trying to open too many accounts and that you won't be able to afford them all.

If lenders such as credit card companies and banks making car or home loans don't like your credit history, they may not trust you enough to loan you money. Or they may decide you are a high risk and loan you money at a higher interest rate than they would if you were a lower-risk customer.

Keeping Your Credit History Clean

Even once you have a credit card, some credit card companies will continue to monitor your credit history to look for your mistakes. A late payment to another company can result in your credit card company hiking your interest rates, even if you've never made a late payment to that company. This is called looking at your credit "purity."

In the last few years, some credit card companies have punished good customers who pay off their bills on time every month by raising interest rates or charging an annual fee. Some credit card companies feel that if they can't earn $25 a year off you in interest, then you should pay $25 a year to them for the privilege of having a card. That's why it's important to pay attention to credit card mailings and watch out for companies changing the terms of your agreement. If you keep your credit history healthy, you should always be able to find a better deal. Let's see what you should look for to find the best credit card deal you can.

Shop around for the best deal on a credit card—different credit companies offer different rates and lines of credit.

Chapter Five

Worth More Than Two Cents: Tips, Pitfalls, and Words of Advice

Michael T. Killian of About.com says that he doesn't recommend that anyone carry a credit card. "Credit cards are like drugs. They offer you short-term pleasure and long-term pain," he says. However, if you are going to have a credit card, Killian suggests that you try to pay off the bill every month or as quickly as you can.

On the other hand, Steve Rhode of Myvesta.org thinks that credit cards are such a handy tool that it's good to have two. He suggests getting one card with the longest grace period you can find, but don't worry about the interest rate on that card. Use that card only for purchases that you can pay off immediately. Rhode suggests getting a second card with the lowest interest rate you can find. Use that card only for big purchases

How to Get the Best Card Deal

Experts say to look for as many of the following as you can:

- ◆ No annual fee—why pay an annual fee if you can get a card that doesn't ask for one?

- ◆ A long grace period—this way, if you do have to carry a balance, you'll get at least the first month interest free.

- ◆ Low interest rate—the lower the interest rate, the less interest you'll have to pay if you do carry a balance. Watch out for low introductory rates that vanish after a few months, and make sure you know what the rate will rise to.

- ◆ No late fee, or low late fee—don't plan on missing a payment, but if you do, the smaller the fee, the better.

that you know you can't pay off all at once. He also suggests doing everything possible not to carry a balance on a credit card.

Rhode also recommends using a credit card instead of a debit card or personal check for catalog or Internet purchases. That way, if you don't like the product or service you received and can't resolve it directly with the merchant, the credit card company will help you fight. However, once you pay with a debit card, the money is gone, and most banks will not want to take the time to help you deal with a surly merchant.

Keep Your Card to Yourself

You should handle your credit cards carefully, not just because you can run up a debt with them, but because other people can steal them and run up bills in your name! If someone else uses your card without your permission, you are responsible for paying the first $50 of the charge, unless you reported the card stolen before it was used. Credit card fraud is common. The cost of credit and charge card fraud was $864 million in 1992, and it is on the rise.

Theft of credit cards themselves is a common fraud, but thieves don't need your card to use your account: They just need the number and expiration date. Thieves can find that information by going through your garbage. Weaselly clerks can even take an extra imprint of your card when you make a purchase at a store. Some thieves steal just your social security number and are able to apply for credit in their names using your good credit history. How can you protect yourself?

• Sign any new card as soon as it arrives.

• Save your receipts, and check them with your billing statements to look for errors.

As soon as you receive a credit card, make sure to sign the back.

- Report any questionable charges to your credit card company as soon as possible. Once you report a lost or stolen card, you are no longer responsible for any unauthorized charges on it. You may be responsible for up to $50 on stolen cards before you report the card lost or stolen.

- Never lend your cards to anyone.

- Never give your credit card information over the phone unless you initiated the call to a company you trust.

- If a card is lost or stolen, report it to your credit card company as soon as possible. Keep all your credit card information in a safe place, away from your credit cards. That way, if a card is stolen, you will have paperwork with contact information.

* Memorize your PIN and never write it down near your credit cards. You don't want someone who steals your wallet to know your secret code.

Staying in Charge of Your Charges

People tend to run into problems with credit cards when they don't pay attention. They don't know how many cards they have, or how much interest they are charged. They use their cards to buy things they can't afford, and before they know it, they are drowning in credit card debt. They can't afford even to make the minimum payment required. They use their credit cards for cash advances to pay bills or buy food, and things continue to spiral out of control as late fees and over-limit fees are added.

Getting a Plan

If you want to keep your finances healthy, you must start with a financial budget. How much money do you make? That's your income. How much money do you spend? Those are your expenses. If you are spending more than you are making, you are running up a debt. If you don't know where your money goes, write down your spending habits. If you spend a $1 a day on soda, you're spending $365 a year on sugar and water. Maybe you would rather spend that money somewhere else.

Most financial advisors will tell you to figure out how much money you are earning and set aside a percentage of that for savings. It can be a third of what you make or only 10 percent. It is important to have a nest egg for emergencies and for big purchases, like buying a car, going to college, or buying a business or home. You can invest your nest egg so it earns interest for you.

Some Words of Wisdom

- **Never take a cash advance.** Both Rhode and Killian say that using credit cards to get a cash advance is foolish. "It's one of the most expensive ways to borrow money," Rhode says.

- **Think before you use your credit card.** Remember, credit cards themselves are the most expensive kind of debt. The average interest charged by credit card companies in 1999 was 17.11 percent. If you use your card, be prepared to pay off your bill as quickly as possible.

- **Ask for special favors**. Competition among credit card companies is so great that once you have established an account with a credit card company, the company may be willing to give you a small favor or two to keep you happy. If your

Think before you use a credit card—don't make purchases that you wouldn't if you had to pay cash.

card charges an annual fee, ask if the company will waive it for you. Ask your credit card company if it can give you a lower interest rate, and threaten to leave if it doesn't. If you do get charged for a late fee, call up and ask for a waiver. Many companies will waive the late fee for good customers. It's not something you can do every month, but it doesn't hurt to try. Credit card companies want to keep their customers and are often willing to give them a break once in a while.

Deals that Sound Too Good

Some credit card companies will lure you to use their cards by offering frequent flier miles or promising to return a percentage of your purchases to you in cash. Sounds like a good deal, right? This is when it is especially important to remember that credit card companies are not your friends. They want to make money off you, and any deal they offer you is going to help them more than you.

Some cash-back offers apply only if you keep a balance, or maintain a constant debt, on your card. And often, anything you get back in cash is less than you paid the company in interest. As for cards that offer frequent flier miles, Killian says that some people may be able to save money, but most will spend more than they save. Watch out for requirements like a high interest rate or an annual fee, plus restrictions on when you can use your miles. It's often better to shop for the best airfare without wasting time trying to use frequent flier miles, which are worth about four cents a mile, Rhode says.

Other cards offer you ways to save on certain products, like new cars or gas. Again, check to be sure you will get the reward even if you don't have a balance, and be sure the reward is something you will actually use.

More Is Not Merrier

The Credit Counseling Centers of America (CCCA) recommends that if you have more than one credit card and are carrying a debt on both or all of them, figure

If there is an error on your bill, write to your credit card company immediately.

out which ones have the lowest rate and transfer all the balances to those, and cancel the ones with the higher interest rates. You will save money by making three payments on three cards instead of ten minimum payments on ten cards. However, you probably don't need more than one or two cards.

Be Organized!

♦ Make sure you pay your bills on time, and don't carry a credit card debt.

♦ Know what your credit card is costing you. Don't be fooled by skipping the fine print. Keep an eye out for a sudden change in terms. Credit card companies can change the terms of their agreements at any time, and they are required to give you only fifteen days notice.

- Know what your credit card limit is, and don't run up a bill to reach it. It's good to have some credit available in case of an emergency, and you don't want to face extra charges for accidentally going over your limit.

- Examine your bills carefully to make sure that there aren't any charges to your account that you don't remember making.

- What can you do if you find an error on your bill? You must write a letter to the credit card company within sixty days of receiving the bill with an error. In your letter, explain why you feel the charge is wrong. The credit card company must investigate the problem and either correct the error or tell you why the bill is correct. It must respond within two billing cycles and not later than ninety days after the company received your letter of complaint.

Less Is Not More

Don't make just the minimum payment. You'll end up paying more in interest than you paid to buy things with the card.

Be a Careful Shopper

It is common for people to spend more on a credit card than they would if they were paying cash. Maybe you'd pay only $30 in cash for a pair of pants, but feel with a credit card, $100 isn't too much to pay. Think about it. You are paying the total amount, plus interest, when you use your card. Don't succumb to the myth of the low monthly payment. Try leaving your credit cards at home when you go shopping. If you see something you must have, take a day or two to think about it.

And never, ever use a cash advance to pay other bills. "You can't borrow your way out of debt," Rhode says. If you find yourself using a cash advance or writing a check on your credit card account to pay other bills, you're in over your head and it's time to seek help.

Asking for Help

What happens if you do run into problems? Don't be afraid to ask for help. Nonprofit centers, like the Credit Counseling Centers of America and Myvesta.org, have counselors who will help you figure out a budget and make arrangements to pay off debts. Instead of struggling with minimum payments you can't make, causing credit card issuers to tack on more late fees, the debt centers will work with your creditors to get your payments to a manageable level. Some centers will work out a plan where you pay them a lump sum every week or month, and they'll send your payment to the creditor. If you are drowning in debt, stop using the cards until you've paid off your debt. Parents, teachers, and other adults can help, too. And watch out for companies that promise to fix your credit problems—for a price. If you are in debt already, adding another bill to the pile is not a good idea.

There aren't enough people teaching teens about spending, laments Steve Rhode. "We live in a society where we are raised to spend, spend, spend," Rhode says. "We look up to people with the best cars, homes, and clothes, and often those people are not more successful, they're just as in debt as everyone else."

Credit is a privilege, not a right. Use yours wisely: Your financial future depends on it!

Glossary

annual fee Amount per year the lender is charging you for having the card, even if you never use it.

annual percentage rate (APR) How much interest will be charged in a year.

automatic teller machine (ATM) Machine that allows customers to withdraw cash using a card and a personal identification number, or PIN.

balance Debt that you owe. It can include fees and interest, not just original purchases.

cash advance Using a credit card to get cash. You can get cash by using your card in an ATM or by writing a check that the credit card company gives you.

cash advance fees Charges a lender levies on you when you use its card in an ATM to get cash or write a check on your credit card account.

charge cards Credit cards that expect you to pay off your balance every month; e.g., American Express.

collateral Something of value that proves you will be able to pay your debt. It can include a home, car, or money deposited in an account.

compound interest Interest calculated on top of interest.

credit cards Cards that are issued by individual banks under a large corporate name, such as Visa, MasterCard, and Discover. Terms and conditions can change depending on the bank that issued the card. The cards work as a loan with a predetermined limit, and come with monthly bills.

credit line Limit of how much money the credit card company is willing to loan to you.

debit cards Cards that are issued by banks in connection with a checking or savings account. You can use a debit card just like a charge card, but instead of loaning you the money, the bank deducts the amount of your purchases from your checking or savings account.

finance charge What it costs to use the card. It can include other charges, such as cash advance fees.

grace period How much time the credit card company allows you to carry a debt without charging interest on it.

guaranteed card Similar to a secured card but usually offered for an application fee through a 900-number.

house cards Credit cards that are good only at the store that issued the card.

interest Percentage of money credit card companies charge to use their cards. It can also refer to the percentage of money you earn if your money is invested.

late charge Fee that a credit card company charges when it doesn't receive your payment by the due date.

limit Dollar amount the company is willing to loan you.

over-the-limit fee Charge levied on you when you spend over your limit.

periodic rate Interest charged in a specific billing period.

personal identification number (PIN) Secret code needed to use debit cards or credit cards at automatic teller machines or in some stores.

principal Dollar amount of your original debt, not including fees or interest.

secured card A card issued by a bank that requires you to make a bank deposit to get the card.

unsecured card Most common type of card, usually just known as a credit card. The bank or issuer of the card doesn't expect you to put up any money up front, and guarantees to loan you a limited amount of money whenever you need it. You sign a contract promising to pay the bills when they come.

Where to
Go for Help

In the United States

Credit Counseling Centers of America
(800) 493-2222
Web site: http://www.cccamerica.com

Federal Trade Commission
CRC-240
Washington, DC 20580
(877) FTC-HELP [382-4357]
Web site: http://www.ftc.gov

Myvesta.org
P.O. Box 8587
Gaithersburg, MD 20898-8587
(800) 680-3328
Web site: http://www.myvesta.org

In Canada

Consumer Credit Counselling
7375 King's Highway, Suite 4
Burnaby, BC V3N 3B5
(604) 526-5155
e-mail: info@iamdebtfree.com

Credit Counselling Society of British Columbia
200–435 Columbia Street
Westminster, BC V3L 5N8
(604) 527-8999
(800) 527-8999

Debt Doktor
Windsor-Essex Office
420 Devonshire Road
Windsor, ON N8Y 4T6
(519) 258-2030
http://www.debtdoktor.org

Personal Credit Counselling Service
Second Floor, Suite 101
Virginia Park Plaza
Newfoundland Drive
St. John's, NF A1A 3E9
(709) 753-5812

Web Sites

About.com
http://www.credit.about.com/finance

Bankrate.com
http://www.bankrate.com/brm/calc/savecalc.asp

Consumer Credit Guide
http://www.creditguide.com

Credit Infocenter
http://www.creditinfocenter.com

DebtWizards.com
http://www.debtwizards.com

Good Money Home Page
http://www.goodmoney.com

Motley Fool for Teens
http://www.fool.com/teens

For Further Reading

Bodnar, Janet. *Mom, Can I Have That? Dr. Tightwad Answers Your Kids' Questions About Money.* Washington, DC: Kiplinger Books, 1996.

Otfinowski, Steve. *The Kid's Guide to Money: Earning It, Saving It, Spending It, Growing It, Sharing It.* New York: Scholastic, 1996.

Pearl, Jayne A. *Kids and Money.* Princeton, NJ: Bloomberg Press, 1999.

Rhode, Steve, and Mike Kidwell. *Get Out of Debt.* Rockville, MD: Debt Counselors of America, 1999.

Stawski, Willard S., III. *Kids, Parents, and Money: Teaching Personal Finance from Piggy Bank to Prom.* New York: John Wiley and Sons, 2000.

Weltman, Barbara. *The Complete Idiot's Guide to Raising Money-Smart Kids.* New York: Alpha Books, 1999.

Index

Index

About the Author

Meg Green is a writer and journalist living in Easton, Pennsylvania. She is also the author of Rosen's *Young Zillionaire's Guide to Saving and Investing*. In her spare time, she enjoys writing fiction, playing the flute, making jewelry, and belly dancing.

Photo Credits

Cover and interior shots by Darren Turner.

Layout

Geri Giordano

www.ingramcontent.com/pod-product-compliance
Lightning Source LLC
Chambersburg PA
CBHW050909210326
41597CB00002B/78